Inspire or Retire
Inspire or Retire
For Teachers by a Teacher

Santiego Rivers

Inspire or Retire

Inspire or Retire

Copyright © 2021 by Santiego Rivers

Editor -

Graphic Designer - Santiego Rivers

Interior Formatting Designer – Santiego Rivers

All rights reserved. No part of this book may be reproduced or transmitted in any form without the written permission of the author.

ISBN 978-1-7352176-7-3

Inspire or Retire

I wrote this book for all overworked, underpaid, and never appreciated teachers and staff members.

This book is my way to say thank you to those teachers and staff members who still manage to touch the lives of their students beyond education and into learning new and exciting things using their unique learning style.

Dedicated educators and staff members are why scholars learn to stop dreaming and become **_dream chasers_**.

Thank you to those educators and staff members who still work as hard as they did when they first started working with adolescents.

Hopefully, your continued passion and effort will inspire your colleagues to re-examine their current methods and philosophy regarding dealing with young and impressionable minds.

> "You are the bows from which your children as living arrows are sent forth."
>
> —KAHLIL GIBRAN

Inspire or Retire

It was a teacher who changed my life. It was that "Highly Effective" and caring educator who replaced the anger and despair of a troubled child with hope and determination never to stop trying to become the best version of themselves.

Having someone to guide me as a youth is why I teach now as an adult. Sharing my testimony with others is why I write. I want to share my stories and touch those of like- minds continue to cherish the responsibility of developing strong minds of their scholars and challenge their peers to do the same for all their scholars.

I am fortunate to have the pleasure of working with some brilliant and bright educators regarding knowledge of the subject. Hopefully, this book can encourage some of my colleagues and maybe yours to consider one essential factor when it comes to giving their scholars the best chance to learn.

"Before you can teach them, you must first learn how to reach them."

"I never teach my pupils. I can only attempt to provide the conditions in which they can learn."

—ALBERT EINSTEIN

Inspire or Retire

New Teachers Beware

Today's Students Vs. Past Students

Teachers with Tenure

Teaching the student & not the subject

What if the scholars you taught were your child?

Equity Issues

What if?

Stuff all good teachers already know:

- School Policy Vs. Classroom Policy
- Getting to know your student
- Understanding the Cultural Differences
- Questions lead to a better understanding
- Bell-to Bell Instructions (Every minute count)

Inspire or Retire

Inspire or Retire

New Teachers Beware

I remember when I first became a Certified Teacher. I took all the lessons that I learned years before to develop a classroom system that I felt would be effective. I have changed them over the years to fit my current students each year.

I remembered the wonderful things my teachers did to make the classroom a "student-centered" environment that fostered learning in many ways.

I remembered having teachers who made it safe to learn despite the many challenges that made learning difficult.

I also took many things that other teachers did that I would not do inside my classroom. I strongly feel that every lesson/ obstacle that we face can serve as a tool for learning.

As new teachers, we all want to develop our teaching style, but we should not re-invent the wheel. We should merely customize the wheel to fit our scholars' needs and not our desires.

The smartest thing that a new teacher can ask anyone who is volunteering them information

Inspire or Retire

about how to "Reach" & "Teach" your scholars is to ask them why they decided to become a teacher themselves?

Let me help ease your mind about me:

My book, **Why I Teach**, could answer the questions you have for me, or any book that I wrote centered towards at-risk-youth will show you where my heart is.

I am not a *"Thank God; it's Friday, Teacher."* I am the type of teacher who plans on the weekend and wakes up each workday without an alarm clock because I love what I do.

My colleagues know that I am not here to make friends. I am here to work. My job is to help scholars become the best version of themselves.

I arrive to work when the Head Plant Operator is opening the door to the school. I am the (PBIS) Positive Behavior Intervention Service at my school. I fund it, which is why my name and company logo are on everything that I do.

I find and provide the money to offer the PBIS activities. I can write a book on just what I do for

Inspire or Retire

my scholars that most educators would say is not in their job description.

I even provide a monthly award service to allow our scholars the opportunity to recognize staff members who they feel went above and beyond their job duties each month. I buy them lunch from restaurants around our area.

Need I say more?

Ask those other advice-givers, do they still have that same passion and drive currently even after teaching for years? How do they reach a child when others have turned their back on them?

Would they *"professionally"* address their colleagues if they saw them treating a child disrespectfully or harming them in any way?

Would they ignore the situation because they don't want to be considered the group's outcast or mess up their *"Work Friendship"*? If they say yes, ask them why are so many "Minority" scholars treated unfairly at your location?

Inspire or Retire

The teachers who you should want as a mentor will have no problem answering these questions. They will be delighted to share this information with you because it is essential to know.

The teachers you should avoid, like COVID-19, will be the ones spreading rumors about you to their little group of "Karen's or Bills."

You know the entitled ones who feel that they are above and beyond everyone else. If you don't know who I'm talking about or have one at your school, you probably are the "Karen or Bill" at your school.

Be sure to have this conversation with your mentor or colleague face to face so that you can see their reaction.

As a new teacher, you will have to ask yourself the question, why do you teach? Do you teach for the salary and the benefits or because you have a desire to help change lives? Changing lives may require you to make some tough sacrifices in your life.

How many lives will you help make better?

Inspire or Retire

Getting to know your student

How can you truly be useful as an educator if you don't understand your students? A few teachers believe that if the students do what they are told, they would learn what they must teach them.

These educators want their students to learn in the way that they teach instead of teaching their scholars in the way that they learn best.

A square peg will never fit into a circle. That does not make the square peg any less than the circle peg. It only makes it different.

If you want your students to learn the information that you are trying to teach them, try doing the following things:

- **Invest in Your Students**
- **Use Humor instead of sarcasm**
- **Vary Your Delivery with your students**
- **Use Behavior Contracts**
- **Get to Know Your Student's Backstory**
- **Use Rewards and Incentives**
- **Just make time to listen to your students**

Inspire or Retire

<u>*Invest time*</u> into getting to know your students. I use the first few minutes of class to find out how my student's day is going and how to make it better.

<u>*Use Humor instead of sarcasm*</u> with your students. It's okay to smile and laugh even at yourself. Show your students that you are human first and a teacher second.

<u>*Vary Your Delivery with your students*</u>. You will have students with different learning ways, so your approach must match many different learning styles.

<u>*Use Behavior Contracts.*</u> Behavior contracts help your students learn to be accountable for their actions and behavior inside your classroom.

Inspire or Retire

Get to Know Your Student's Backstory. Many of the behavior and anger issues that your student brings into your classroom are not about you. The behavior and anger issues that your lack of connecting with your students bring are totally on you. Please take a moment to teach your students how to take a moment for themselves and reset their day.

Use Rewards and Incentives. As educators, your paycheck is your incentive for you to come to work each day. Why not give small incentives to help motivate your students to stay on task and learn?

Just make time to listen to your students. I am a big fan of student surveys and creating vision boards to connect with my students. Whether I am teaching inside the classroom or working as a Behavior Specialist, I make time to listen.

The few minutes you take to get to know your students could save you weeks and months of dealing with behavior issues inside your classroom.

Just a suggestion...

Inspire or Retire

Today's Students Vs. Past Students

I hear many of my colleagues talk about how different students of today are compared to the students we currently have. To be transparent, each generation before us becoming a teacher could say the same thing about their students.

Many of my colleagues feel that things went downhill when we took out having or doing certain things in schools, from prayers to the paddle and ruler discipline our educators gave us.

The changes are many, but the effects have drastically changed how teachers teach and how students learn.

In the past, students were sat down and told to memorize the information of subjects. Now the curriculum has expanded and makes students work in groups to compare, contrast, and discuss topics to increase their knowledge. Scholars now work on their communication skills. The change in the curriculum will help their future more than knowing facts. Unfortunately, many educators are still using the sample principles to educate our scholars.

Inspire or Retire

Educators must now go to professional development training to learn how to adjust their classroom to fit into the often-changing curriculum and how our students learn.

Many of those teachers ignore all the information taught in the professional development training. They return to their classroom with the same mindset.

These same teachers are upset when their students display the same attitude or discontent, they show to their supervisor each day by not following the schools' policy sticking with their classroom rules, often like their home rules.

This discontent for following the rules is often found in two types of teachers—those who teach for the wrong reasons and those educators who are grand-fathered into their contracts.

(Teachers with Tenure)

Inspire or Retire

Teachers with Tenure

There are both good and bad when it comes to teachers having tenure in their profession. Teacher tenure exists for two fundamental reasons:

to protect educators from political or personal retribution and guarantee their academic freedom to teach according to their expertise fields' best practices.

Tenure ensures the administration cannot fire **good teachers** for their race, gender, age, religion, handicapping, or sexual orientation.

Tenure ensures that **the administration cannot fire good teachers** because of local politics. It ensures they cannot be terminated for pregnancy.

Tenure protects teachers from being fired for teaching unpopular, controversial, or otherwise challenged curricula. Tenure helps with recruitment because it offers teachers a stable and secure job.

Tenure gives teachers the freedom to be creative in the classroom and rewards them for their years of dedication.

Inspire or Retire

Tenure also ensures that those who have been there longest have guaranteed job security in tough economic times.

Let us look at some of the negative when it comes to tenure for educators.

Teacher tenure leads to complacency because teachers know they are not likely to lose their employment. Why would anyone go above and beyond their job duty when they do not have to?

Tenure makes it costly for schools to remove a teacher with poor performance or guilty of wrongdoing.

Administrators are less likely to discipline a tenured teacher than a probationary teacher even if they have committed the same offense because it is such a difficult proposition to remove a tenured teacher.

The students suffer in situations like this, and good educators are forced to be judged by their colleagues' actions.

Inspire or Retire

Teaching the student & not the subject

As I mentioned earlier in this book, I know some brilliant teachers regarding knowledge of the subject area.

These brilliant teachers have master's Degrees, and some of these educators have Ph.D.'s attached to their names.

These educators can talk hours on end about many different subjects while giving you their personal opinions on each matter.

When it comes to the curriculum, these teachers are wizards and have taken many district trainings to stay abreast with the latest updates in their field.

These educators have a wealth of knowledge, but unfortunately, many cannot deliver it to their students.

Scholars can find the knowledge of the curriculum in books or online to obtain an education. Still, real learning happens when the pupil can grasp the information that registers in their brain.

Inspire or Retire

Learning for most scholars may require these brilliant and highly educated teachers "dumbing-down" their delivery on how they teach their scholars.

When a parent is teaching their toddler, they break down the information/ things they want them to learn in a way that makes sense to them. Why can't you use that same philosophy with your scholars?

What good is having all the knowledge in the world if you lack the wisdom to share it in a way that allows the attended audience to receive it?

Sometimes we must help our scholars re-establish or even establish a foundation of the subject area to grasp the information you are trying to teach them.

Yes, I know that our current curriculum does not allow room for teaching information that our scholars were supposed to learn in previous years. Still, I have a straightforward question for all educators and staff members. If the attended audience was your son or daughter, would you take the time or find ways to make sure that you helped them obtain the missing information needed to be successful?

Inspire or Retire

What if the scholars you taught were your child?

To all my educators and staff members who work with young adults, I want to ask you a straightforward question.

If the scholars you taught or worked with were your son or daughter, would you treat them in the same manner you treat individual scholars that you feel makes your job more difficult?

Most of you would quickly say you would treat your current scholars the same way you would your kids, but unfortunately for many of you, that is not accurate.

I can't see you allowing your kids to struggle in an area you are very knowledgeable about. I also can't see you writing referrals and suspending your child when you can have conferences with them and use many other resources to get them back on track.

A few educators may claim to use tough love on their child, but is that just a way of saying that maybe you lack in have compassion? Hopefully, if you don't see this as a human compassion issue, you have been taught about **"equity issues"**?

Inspire or Retire

Equity Issues

Many schools offer "Equity" training" for their staff each year to better understand the importance of equity being used in our schools.

The main problem with "Equity Training" is that it is voluntary and not mandatory for all staff members.

The lack of equity understanding for people who work with children is a form of mental child abuse in my eyes. Child abuse training is required each year for staff members in my district, so why not equity?

I know that a staff member taking an equity class will not change who they are as a person, but it can be a paper trail to terminate them for knowingly abusing a child mentally.

Let us get a better understanding of what equity is as it relates to our education system. In education, the term "equity" refers to the principle of fairness. Equity helps all students develop the knowledge and skills they need to be engaged in school and become productive members of society.

Inspire or Retire

While equality means treating every student the same, equity means making sure every student has the support they need to be successful. Equity in education requires putting systems in place to ensure that every child has an equal chance for success.

Equity does not mean that you treat one student better than the other. Equity means that you assure your students can learn in a way that makes sense to them.

There is so much _systematic racism_ in our schools it is pathetic. You can find it within the curriculum, the State testing, and even within the staff members who are supposed to help our scholars.

At my school alone, I know of a staff member with the title of an "Equity Champion," but she is far from it. She is very knowledgeable in her work, but her entitled ways and how she picks and chooses to decide which students deserve to be treated fairly by her and her work friends is not what I consider an "Equity Champion."

I could go on & on about her and some other people who fail our students each day, but I will digress and leave you with this. **(Romans 12:19, KJV)**

Inspire or Retire

What if?

What if the scholars sitting before you inside the classroom were your son or daughter? Would you take the extra time to make sure that they understood the assignment you taught in a way that makes sense to them? Would you re-teach lessons that did not register to them outside of their learning style?

Would you take the time to see what's going on inside their minds when they're acting out or shutting out everything around them? Would you make time to do what is in the scholar's best interest when there is no time?

These are just a few of the questions that I would like to ask my colleagues who struggle to make a "Human" connection with their students inside their classroom. Maybe some of their scholars' parents would like to ask their child's teachers some questions.

These are the Teachers who regularly make behavior calls on students and request discipline referrals quicker than they would take a moment to see what is going on with the child.

Inspire or Retire

Yes, many of your scholars who look like adults are still children. Teachers might want to post the following quote inside their classroom:

"If you want to be treated as an adult, you should act like an adult."

Educators and Staff members will be required to do the same thing; act like an adult. Stop taking everything kids say to you so personally. The main difference between the things that kids say and adults say is that adults hold onto the negative for an extended time.

When students say hurtful and mean words, they have the capability of getting over it quicker than most adults. As an educator, I have struggled with this lesson until I learned to stop taking the things kids say so personally.

"Don't take things so personally."

It is hard to learn, but the benefits outweigh the struggle; it takes your pride to accept the benefits.

Inspire or Retire

Stuff all good teachers already know:

- School policy Vs. Classroom practice
- Getting to know your student
- Understanding the Cultural Differences
- Questions lead to a better understanding
- Bell-to Bell Instructions **(Every minute count)**

Classroom practice should be aligned with the school policy where you work. Home rules do not work at your worksite.

There are far too many teachers treating their classrooms like their homes regarding how they deal with their scholars. Situations like this occur despite the school policy outlined in their handbook. Sometimes the school policy is posted around the schools in many cases.

Getting to know your students and their individual needs will help you ensure that you are doing everything possible to make sure that you are providing them with the opportunity to learn in a way that works best. **(Learning Styles)**

Inspire or Retire

<u>Understand the cultural differences between your students</u>. African American students may ask many questions that can be frustrating to educators trying to teach through lectures.

Here is a simple way to help you with this:

Today, I will be teaching you a lesson about life. This conversation may leave you with questions. Some of your questions may be answered as I teach the class. Please hold your questions until the end, and I will be sure to answer them.

You can write your questions down so you can remember them all. I will leave time between teaching to allow you the opportunity to answer a few of your questions.

<u>Questions lead to a better understanding</u>. Inventors invent, and Scientists discover things because they have questions.

People who think outside of the box tend to ask a lot of questions. Most educators fail to realize that if students ask you questions about the lesson, they are probably paying attention.

Inspire or Retire

<u>Bell-to-Bell instructions</u> are among the best ways to reduce behavior problems inside your classroom and help keep your scholars on task.

You can start your class by allowing your scholars to demonstrate what they learned the following day or answering questions that students left behind in the 'exit box" the previous day.

You can allow your scholars to put their questions about today's lesson inside the "Exit Box" at the end of each class.

Bell-to-Bell instructions do not mean that you spend all class lecturing to your scholars. The person who talks the most learns the most. Your class should be student lead as they explore new ideas.

Inspire or Retire

Inspire or Retire

Teachers can be ineffective for a variety of reasons. Some have a weak grasp of the material or are tough to understand by their students.

Other ineffective teachers are bad at controlling and directing their class. They are weak when it comes to classroom management.

Teachers can be too aggressive or too passive when it comes to their students. Being bold does not work with most students.

An ordinary teacher can fail to inspire their students. A bad teacher can damage a student's confidence and self-perception of themselves.

Students can grow to doubt their abilities and lash out negatively from dealing with ineffective teachers.

For these reasons alone, I say the following:

From the bottom of my heart, I wish that all educators and staff members who have lost

Inspire or Retire

the passion for what they do would retire from the teaching profession.

I am speaking for myself and on behalf of all the student's lives that you encounter daily in a negative way.

Athletes know when to hang it up when the desire or ability is gone; why not you? You poison the people around you with your negative behavior and actions.

You destroyed futures when your job was to build and give hope to your scholars. You are part of the school system's problem and how parents and students view all of us.

Your dinosaur way of thinking and personal bigot ways of acting serves no purpose in the workforce. At least a bad cop can be viewed by others as doing some good with their presence to help detour crime.

An ineffective teacher is only effective when they don't show up for work. You make my stomach and A** hurt just thinking about you destroying a child's life.

Inspire or Retire!!!

Inspire or Retire

Reference Page

- Watanabe-Crockett, L. (2020, January 22). *10 Inspirational Education Quotes for Educators Everywhere*. Wabi-sabi Learning. https://wabisabilearning.com/blogs/mindfulness-wellbeing/10-inspiring-teaching-quotes

- education-now-vs-20-years-ago. (2021, February 13). Tttoday.Com. https://tttoday.comaf/3032/columns/education-now-vs-20-years-ago/#:~:text=Twenty%20years%20ago%2C%20education%20was,for%20a%20project%20or%20research.&text=One%20major%20difference%20that%20has,students%20skills%20instead%20of%20content.

- what-is-teacher-tenure. (n.d.). Www.Thoughtco.Com. Retrieved February 14, 2021, from https://www.thoughtco.com/what-is-teacher-tenure-3194690

- the-long-term-effects-of-ineffective-teachers. (n.d.). Www.Brooklynmathtutors.Com. Retrieved February 14, 2021, from https://www.brooklynmathtutors.com/the-long-term-effects-of-ineffective-teachers#:~:text=Teachers%20can%20be%20ineffective%20for,controlling%20and%20directing%20their%20class.